How Many Lies Are Too Many?

Learn How to Spot Con Artists, Pathological Liars, Cheaters, Narcissists and Psychopaths Before They Spot You

Learn How to Recognize Gaslighting in Your Relationship

Part of the "Gaslight Survivor" Series

Victoria Summit

Victoria Summit

Special Thanks to Suzanne B.

All content is copyright protected in all forms and media and may not be reproduced in any form without express written permission from Victoria Summit and/or Scarlett Publishing.

The author and publishing company advise for anyone in a trauma, crisis or going through emotional upheaval, to seek advice from a qualified professional.

Information in this book is opinion and entertainment only. Characters are fictional although based on real-life cases.

Copyright 2013 Victoria Summit
Copyright 2013Dreamstime 2013 Lina0486

Published by Scarlett Publishing

April 2013

How Many Lies Are Too Many?

Contents

WHY WRITE ANOTHER LIAR BOOK? 5

HOW MANY LIES ARE TOO MANY? 7

HOW TO RECOGNIZE GASLIGHTING IN YOUR RELATIONSHIP 9

TRUSTING OURSELVES 11

ABUSIVE BEHAVIOUR 15

GETTING GASLIGHTED 16

AT WHAT POINT DID THE RELATIONSHIP GROW SOUR 17

GASLIGHT IS EVERYWHERE 18

IT'S A GASLIGHT WORLD 20

VILLAINS 22

MALIGNANT NARCISSISTIC PERSONALITY DISORDER 23

THREE PHASES OF GASLIGHTING 26

SPOTTING THE CRACKS IN THE ARMOR 28

NO CONTACT	30
GASLIGHT SHAME	32
EXAMPLES OF GASLIGHTING LIES	34
BEWARE OF LIARS	37
ABOUT THE AUTHOR	40

How Many Lies Are Too Many?

Why Write Another Liar Book?

There are dozens if not hundreds of books in the world warning people about liars and cheaters. It seems like no matter how many books are written, the liars and cheaters still have the power to destroy lives.

I've worked with hundreds of clients over the years, helping them to see the red flags in relationships and encouraging them to find the courage to leave a dysfunctional relationship.

It seems to me that people source out books when they have a gut feeling something isn't right or they can't put their finger on what exactly is wrong. Sometimes people know they are with a pathological liar and want to read as much as they can about the subject. People in pain often seek out stories from other people who have gone through the same thing. In the human experience, we want to know that we are not alone.

You are not the first person to be the target of a liar. You will always be a target as will I and anyone else. You have to get smart at not listening to lies, don't believe tears and watch for actions not words.

Actions define who a person really is. Actions from how that person lives his life, to how he treats family and friends, how he treats animals and how he treats exes and his own children.

Someone who blames others for his life choices is not a healthy person to be around. Someone who lies and manipulates to seemingly impress you or "protect" you is not a person you should hook your life, home and finances with for any length of time.

In this day and age of identity theft and lying desperation, a private investigator or criminal background check will be worth the investment.

Victoria Summit

I'm hoping that people reading this book and my other books will realize that they are not alone, that we all give the wrong people the benefit of the doubt sometimes and that we all can find the courage to cut the losers out of our lives and move on to better and more productive living.

If your life is more drama than living, you might be involved with a liar or a gaslighter.

How Many Lies Are Too Many?

Is it ever okay to tell a lie?

Is it ever okay to accept a lie?

You need to ask yourself, why are you letting your lover lie to you? What is missing in your life that you are willing to accept a man or woman who doesn't think twice about lying to your face?

If you have an ache in your gut that something isn't quite right then it probably isn't.
If your partner shows no remorse in the lies he or she tells you, how can you ever trust him or her?

Trust is the basis of your relationship.

You only get one chance at life. How do you want to spend it?

How many lies are too many?

Is every word out of your lover's mouth a bold faced lie?

Are there only lies when he or she wants his or her own way?

Are there lies about where your sweetie has been or where he or she is going?

When caught in a lie, does your sweetie come clean or lie on top of the lies?

When do the lies stop?

Victoria Summit

Like the boy who cried wolf, there will come a point where you won't be able to tell where the lies begin and end. If you end up going this far in a relationship, you may well be getting gaslighted so that your sweetie can get away with the lies. Protect yourself and protect your heart. See the lies for what they really are.

Your sweetie doesn't respect you nor does he or she love you. If there is love, there are no lies. It's very simple.

Ask yourself, why do you stay? Why do you put up with the lies? Where is your self-respect?

If you're frightened of your lover, you need to phone the police, get a counsellor, call a hotline, get a lawyer, contact a woman's shelter or a mentor. No matter your age and income, there is help to get you out of an abusive situation. You need to make the first step to help yourself which is recognizing that you are being lied to and you need to remove yourself from this relationship as soon as you can and as smoothly as you can.

How Many Lies Are Too Many?

How to Recognize Gaslighting in Your Relationship

Gaslight is a term used to describe lies and the manipulative behaviour that goes with them.
Gaslighting occurs when someone (the Gaslighter) manipulates reality to suit his or her own personal needs and convinces the other person (the Gaslightee) that the Gaslighter's version of events is true even when the Gaslightee suspects or even knows that it isn't but wants to please the Gaslighter, often in an attempt to avoid violent outbursts.

Before long, the sense of true reality and trust of "self" for the gaslightee becomes eroded. Reality is skewed and the lines between reality and lies blur more every day. The modern day usage of the term comes from the Alfred Hitchcock movie, "Gaslight" and is readily used by psychiatrists to describe a specific behavior that abusers use to control their victims.

A lie is a lie. There is no excuse for lying. Opinions vary if lying is acceptable if it spares one's feelings.

However those aren't the lies being discussed in this book.

These lies are the ones that make you wonder if you're losing your mind.

These lies target your memory, your patience, your perception of reality, and your sense of sanity.

Gaslighting is outright manipulation. This can include actually rearranging furniture, resetting clocks to different times, erasing and retyping messages, hiding objects and then having them "reappear," double talk, drugging the victim, showing faked phone records, faked receipts, faked paychecks, faked bank accounts, convincing other people to lie for them and using other means to control the victim.

Gaslighting often happens very gradually and over a period of time. It will start with little things but eventually it will feel like you don't know what's true and what isn't anymore. In fact, you do know what is reality but you're screamed at and bullied so much when you act upon the real facts that you start to blur the line between fantasy and reality and lose trust in your own perception.

Stand strong to the gaslighter. This may mean leaving as soon as you can. This also means that once you've left, have zero contact with your gaslighter. After all, why do you need to speak with your gaslighter? You already know every word out of his or her mouth is a pack of lies anyways.

Don't waste your time. Don't lament the life, money, home, friends, and so on that you've lost. The reality is you can build again. It won't be easy but getting away and starting your life over is the best gift you can give to yourself. You also will be setting an excellent example for your children about how not to let yourself be bullied and controlled.

Once you recognize what is going on and you leave, you can only be grateful that you left.

If you recognize what is going on and you stay, you are not setting a good example for your children and your friends will slowly leave you. Don't be a victim. No money, no house, nothing is worth being lied to and screamed at every day.

Peace of mind and peace of heart is what you need and you'll never get it under the same roof as a gaslighter.

How Many Lies Are Too Many?

Trusting Ourselves

Why don't some of us trust our "gut feelings?" Why do we excuse "strange behaviour" hoping that things will get better? How can we determine if our hearts are being conned before it's too late?
Most people have had relationships that didn't work out for a variety of reasons. Boredom, lack of common interest, incompatible sex drive, growth in different directions, and so on. Those relationships can be roller coasters and most relationships don't end on a happy note but some can be downright amicable. That's life and we all move on. No one should ever feel bad about taking a chance in life and hoping for the best. Sometimes people are only meant to meet for a short time before moving on to find more long term situations.

However, there can be a darker side to some relationships. Circumstances appear perfect or normal on the outside but behind closed doors, there's something sinister going on.

Yet many women and men ignore early gut feelings and red flags thinking this can't possibly be happening to them. They expect evil to look more obvious. They forget all their lessons and fairy tales because they believe in love and compassion and if they really try, everything will work out okay. They don't believe that many books and movies are based on real-life stories, that serial killers walk among us, that the Marquis De Sade is alive and well. As the tornado begins to spin in their lives, confusion grows, and escape becomes a monumentally difficult task both emotionally and physically. Each day the lies take hold with their unflinching hooks becomes another day enmeshed in emotional and physical entanglement that can take months or even years to escape.

If a person is grounded in a realistic and healthy sense of self, then the antics of a Gaslighter won't get very far. He or she will recognize the lies or at the very least, feel like something is "off" early on. Someone who has a strong sense of self-worth won't contort to the whims of a narcissist although it is surprising how many people in "power" careers or heritage can become victims as well.

If something inside of you starts to niggle when you're listening to yet another excuse about why your beloved is arriving home late, listen to your aching stomach, watch his eyes glancing away and upwards as he fabricates his webs of deceit. Some Gaslighters will be certain to stare you down to make you doubt yourself. Don't fall for it. Stay grounded in what YOU think, not what is in his bullying behaviour.

People who are strong won't put up with the Gaslighter and can diffuse the games before it's too late. Everyone has his or her own barometer of what is tolerable behavior. The Gaslighter preys on the patient and nurturing people of the world. Although he may well eventually destroy their gentle nature and create grand disillusionment in human nature, sometimes for life. In the meantime, he'll target the emotional core of the compassionate while weaving tales of how the world has wronged him and that's why he gets angry or cheats or steals or kills. Don't believe that you can make this wounded puppy better. You can't.

To make certain that you're not falling under the spell of a Gaslighter or a pathological liar, take a hard look at your life today. Right now.

Are you doing what you should be?
Are you following your own dreams or did somehow along the way, you start to live your sweetie's dreams?
Do you worry about "making a mistake?"
Do you dress how your sweetie **wants** you to, especially to avoid arguments?
Did you change your hairstyle or colour or manner of dress because your sweetie **told** you to?
Are you doing more giving than taking?
Are you accused of having a distorted view of sex even though you just want what you had all along until somewhere along the way, the rules changed?

How Many Lies Are Too Many?

Do you go to bed sad?
Do you fall asleep alone?
Do you dread your sweetie coming home from work?
Do you wonder which "personality" of your sweetie will arrive home from work?
Are you walking on eggshells?
Do you have to "happy talk" yourself to get up in the morning?
Did you used to be happy and now you're not?
Does something feel "off" but you can't put your finger on it?
Are things "too good to be true?"
Are you being pressured to sign legal documents?
Are you being pressured to marry after a short time together?
Are you in a better tax bracket than your sweetie?
Do you own property?
Do you dread social events?
Do you find yourself lying for your sweetie's behavior?
Do you make excuses for your sweetie?
Are you often told that you make stuff up when you're 100% certain you know the truth?
Are you having physical issues such as backaches and migraines?
Are you on the verge of a stroke?
Do you have stomach aches? Ulcers? Acid reflux?
Do you burst into tears for no reason?
Do you question your own memory?
Do you think you're becoming forget ful?
Are your thoughts "murky" and disjointed?
Have you stopped attending events you used to enjoy because your mate doesn't want you to?
Does your mate belittle you and call you stupid?
Are you suddenly "incompetent" even though you managed to get yourself through life before meeting your mate?

Any and all of these are ideas to consider if you think you're dealing with a Gaslighter, Narcissist, Con Artist or Cheater.

People with healthy self-esteem will tailor lives that benefit their mind, body and souls. They know what's best for themselves and their families and won't become manipulated into performing activities outside of their basic moral character.

Life is short. Every day is a gift. Be grateful for each life lesson for there's a new day, a new hour, a new minute right in front of you ready to be explored.

How Many Lies Are Too Many?

Abusive Behaviour

Abuse can take many forms and some of them are obvious. One or both partners can have issues with drugs, alcohol, gambling, sex addictions, power struggles, cheating, childhood or sexual abuse, trauma, and so on. There can be physical and mental abuse that is easily identified by professionals and everyday people.

But there are other types of abuse and co-dependency that are insidious, that can creep into our lives without us realizing it. Types of abuse that aren't recognized as readily as the "wife beater" or "gambler" or "the alcoholic," or "the cheater," that people don't really talk about and aren't as well known in the media in all its forms except the most extreme cases that become highlighted for our amusement.

Even trained professionals such as psychiatrists, lawyers, and judges might not diagnose or detect these people. In fact, many trained professionals are these people too.

Narcissists, Con Artists, Cheaters and Psychopaths all use their charm and gas lighting techniques to get what they want from life. As with any behaviour, we all need survival skills but at what point does survival of the fittest mean destroy your fellow man?

Since always.

And that's what "Nice" people have to remember. Some people don't deserve the benefit of a doubt. It pays to learn how to spot liars from the start.

Getting Gaslighted

When first meeting a Gaslighter, the Gaslightee can be enamoured, hormones in overdrive, dancing with the devil who mirrors our darkest fantasies, that man who knows the perfect words to whisper in our ear, the woman who seduces our imagination like no woman ever has, so we're not thinking straight. Blinded by love, by lust, by the joy of companionship. We've found our soulmate and nothing can harm us now.

In reality, the Gaslighter had spotted you and laid out his trap long before you even knew he was aware of your existence.

The Gaslighter has studied you, has listened so attentively to your wants and needs so he can mirror them in the beginning and then withhold them once you're under his or her spell.

The Gaslightee is in fact living every inch of fantasy come true, whatever that may mean, and all the friends and family love the new lover, the Gaslighter. Almost everyone loves the Gaslighter, (there will be a few savvy friends who can spot the wolf in sheep's clothing but may not be sure what to say so stay quiet) yet somehow as time goes on, the Gaslightee develops an aching sense of "something isn't right" but can't quite identify what is wrong. Their natural glow of enthusiasm towards life is slowly being worn away and the Gaslightee grows confused and angry, living in a fog, unable to make decisions, crying for no reason, and ultimately end up screaming like a lunatic in endless pointless arguments that last for hours.

The Gaslighter and Gaslightee are in a tango, an ebb and flow of supply and demand. Often, both parties can be abusive if the relationship isn't stopped. Anger feeds anger and when head games are played daily, exhaustion and self-doubt can lead to behaviour beyond the norm for both parties.

At What Point Did The Relationship Grow Sour

Everything starts off great. You've been lonely for a long time, perhaps you're divorced, have kids, inherited a lot of money, own your own home, have a generous spirit, might be struggling or might be doing really well. You might even be a very powerful judge, lawyer, doctor or celebrity.

This lovely person enters your life, filling those pockets of sadness and loneliness. Suddenly after all those dark days, this vision of light and love and good floods your world. Your every wish is granted, your sex life has never been so hot, and there may even be an engagement or move-in within the first few months.

Then somehow, it all falls off the rails. Suddenly, days are filled with dread and arguments, sleeping alone and crying in the night.

What happened? When did this happen and how did this happen? There were no obvious signs that life wouldn't be perfect with this partner.

Or were there?

Gaslight Is Everywhere

We live in a "Gaslight" society. There's always been "gaslighting" around and most of us do a mild version of it to someone at some time or another, but there's a line and when it's crossed, there's a huge level of deceit going on.

We can be gaslighted by lovers, parents, children, relatives, friends, bosses, coworkers; anyone who has some sort of influence in our lives. Gaslighting is where someone manipulates reality to suit his or her own personal needs and convinces the other person that the gaslighter's version of events is true when the gaslightee often knows it isn't but wants to please the gaslighter and before long, the sense of true reality and trust of "self" become eroded.

Gaslight Survivors include women and men, teenagers, children. It doesn't matter who you are or how old you are, you need to spot the gaslighters, cheaters, and narcissists in your life and disengage from these unproductive, dysfunctional, and volatile relationships. There is only pain and no gain when you tango with a narcissist; loss of self, financial disaster, and sometimes even the loss of your own natural children can all be part of the final act. People who break free of gaslighting relationships are Gaslight Survivors.

Red flags and unacceptable behavior patterns may seem obvious to most people, but there are other people, sometimes very well educated people with powerful careers, who are perfect magnets for narcissists who love to gaslight.

The gaslighting behaviour pattern needs to be taught to susceptible people before they get in too deep. We need to show the general population that this isn't a matter of accepting eccentric idiosyncrasies with a "troubled" or "artistic" or "genius" man or woman. Narcissist Personality Disorder is a dangerous mental condition that can result in

How Many Lies Are Too Many?

physical demise and financial ruin. It's not only "stupid, desperate" people who fall for these con artists of the heart and mind. In fact, it's often the other way around. Information needs to be given to young people so that they don't grow up performing in a dance macabre.

It's fine to have self-esteem, be proud of who you are, even strive to be a superstar, but it's how you treat other people that defines you.

Someone who gaslights chronically is selfish at the very least and dangerous at the very worst.

It's A Gaslight World

Since the fifties we've lived in a gaslight world; a bombardment of conflicting media, lying officials, corrupt social enforcers, online social networking, philandering celebrities, and so on.

As woman's lib evolved, women tried to be independent but often tried to please the man more than woman in earlier times did, to compensate for the guilt of working. A new generation of narcissistic men were born. But just because someone is self-absorbed or spoiled doesn't mean that he or she will become or is a Gaslighter. However, the person who truly has narcissistic personality disorder will use gaslighting as a favorite tool of manipulation in the old toolbox.

Some of the most popular shows right now feature gaslighting and narcissists. Dexter, Californication, Twilight, True Blood, even Big Love. Don't get me started on Narcissistic Kody on "Sisterwives." Inception was a huge hit and in the end, one big gaslight. Horror movies, comic books, and mysteries almost always feature narcissists and gaslighting.

Who is Count Dracula but a gaslighter, a narcissist, a psychopath, a serial killer?

How about Dorian Gray, a narcissist who had traits of hedonism and entitlement? He has to gaslight everyone about how he doesn't age and hide the portrait that ages for him.

Jekyll and Hyde has a mad scientist with self-inflicted bi-polar disease who has to gaslight the world around him to keep his murderous secrets.

Dr. Frankenstein plays God and had to gaslight even his fiancé to keep his despicable animated corpse secret. A narcissist, who has no thought for anyone around him and even in his remorseful diary, is still arrogant.

How Many Lies Are Too Many?

The Wizard of Oz gaslighted an entire kingdom.

Many childhood myths and rituals require gaslighting a child. Santa Claus is one of the biggest gaslighting cults on the planet. Entire countries perpetrate a myth that a man flies around the world in a sled driven by flying reindeer giving out free toys made by slave labour elves in a castle at the North Pole. Some would argue that some organized religions use gas lighting techniques to suspend belief in the "magic" of miracles and the truth of fables presented as documented evidence. Any situation that requires the truth as you see it, being told to you that it isn't the truth at all, could be considered gaslighting.

Gaslighting makes for excellent entertainment as we've seen by our tiny sampling.

However, gaslighting is not so entertaining when it's burning out of control in your own personal life.

Villains

Of course, there have always been narcissists. We can see glaring examples throughout history. We know about ruthless rulers and unsolved serial killings. Almost every TV show from 48 Hours to 20/20 profiles serial killers and con artists at some point.

The best villains are the ones with smarts and charisma. Remember the serial killer Ted Bundy was supposedly one handsome and charming man. Many villains in stories are cunning, seductive, ruthless, predatory and pathological liars.

Stories are stories, yes. And stories are created by human writers who think them up and write them down. Writers record the human experience whether they are making it up in their heads or basing their ideas on research or even familiar haunts and people. Once you realize that evil can really and truly be right there on the couch beside you, then it's easier to recognize it.

It's human nature to be an ostrich. Put our heads in the sand and don't rock the boat. Especially once the sweetie in your life starts to turn sour. Don't be an ostrich. Don't give the benefit of the doubt. Adults need to be accountable for their own behaviour. No work day is so rough that any man or woman needs to come home and scream at the spouse and kids. No life is healthy and productive if every day is filled with stress, waiting for time bombs to go off. Don't let the first lie slip by or you'll be creating a dangerous precedent.

As the population has grown, so has the amount of people who are out to get you are out there. This isn't a paranoid delusion, it's statistics. Awareness needs to be made to share information about these people; that they are real, not just our entertainment, so that the inevitable nightmare of tangoing with one can be avoided. Smoke and mirrors isn't just in Las Vegas.

How Many Lies Are Too Many?

Malignant Narcissistic Personality Disorder

Both men and women can have Malignant Narcissistic Personality Disorder. It is also called Psychopath.

Not all narcissists use gaslighting as a strategy but the ones who do are as close to evil on earth as you can get without bursting into flame. Gaslighting is a popular technique used by abusers to keep their victims confused, on edge and under their control.

4% of the population have Narcissistic Personality Disorder (NPD) of the dangerous kind. This means that there are millions of them walking around right this very minute. All of us have narcissism to some degree; it's a survival of the fittest world. These are people with the most extreme cases.

As babies, we are all total narcissists, waited on hand and foot. We continue to be narcissists until early adulthood when we learn that the world doesn't revolve around us and we have to adapt to societies' constraints to fit in and live productively. The majority of people figure out how to best fit into the unique and specific social and moral parameters of modern society in some way or another.

Narcissists (Ns) don't adapt. They are like Peter Pan, refusing to grow up and have healthy mature relationships. They are stuck forever in the pre-teen world of irresponsibility.

Ns believe that they are special and that society's rules don't apply to them. They expect preferential treatment and break the rules wherever they can by having affairs, manipulating other people's financial matters or worse. They are charmers, manipulative, cunning, are prone to fits of rage, and are usually the best sex you'll ever have. Narcissists don't have much of a conscience if any. This is how they can pretend to love you or care about you and not feel guilt about lying. They are missing an important component. Empathy. The Narcissist, Psychopath and Sociopath can't imagine putting themselves into someone else's shoes. They blame everyone else for anything that is wrong in their own lives.

The first few months or even years, (depending on their plan for you), with an N is a fairy tale come true. They shower you with affection, presents, have the same interests as you, are often romantic, will do special things, often propose quickly, give you the best sex you ever had and so on. He (or she) is mirroring your every desire and delivering it in abundance. You are seduced, thinking you've found your soul mate.

Then suddenly, for no reason, the tables turn. Once the N has you securely under his spell, he is often already on to his next victim behind your back. Ns are notorious cheaters though not all cheaters have NPD. You don't realize he is straying or if you have gut feelings you are met with tears or rage whenever you question what is going on. You believe the tears and duck from the rage and life goes on.

Ns cannot love, not like the rest of us do. They are arrested in some sort of infantile development loop and act like screaming toddlers with a temper tantrum when angry and run around like promiscuous teenagers when bored, which they always are since they have no sense of passion or follow through. Ns can be procrastinators, jealous, possessive, secretive, careless with your money, have job issues, blame others for their problems, and have odd habits which are amazingly consistent once you start talking to other people who have tangoed with Ns.

Full blown Ns cannot give or receive love, feel no guilt, think they are special, blame everyone else for their problems, have no compassion, are greedy with money and sex, obsessed with conquests of all kinds, are jealous, and quick to anger. They can never be cured because in the majority of cases, this is a neurological disorder. Sometimes narcissistic behavior is learned as a child from a parent and if it's learned, it can be sometimes be "fixed" somewhat with years of therapy. But most cases are likely genetic although researchers still don't have all the answers.

How Many Lies Are Too Many?

One of the reasons Ns can't be cured relates to the fact they likely don't believe they have a mental illness or they waste everyone's time by mirroring the therapist or gaslighting her instead of actually "working." The Ns may go to therapy for a while and deem themselves cured and be on their way. Ns cannot change their behaviour nor do they want to or feel they have to nor do they care. They are wired the way they are wired and it can be devastating for those who love them to realize that the N cannot change. No amount of therapy will teach the N love or how to experience compassion for anyone, including themselves. Some of the milder cases can be taught behaviour skills to cope in relationships and some of these people have even written about being narcissists and how they learn to adapt to society and have relationships. "Malignant Self-Love" by Dr. Sam Vaknin is an excellent book written by a narcissist. He has hundreds of articles about NPD posted on the Internet that are eye-opening and valuable reading. All of his books are must-reads on the subject. He explains, as a malignant narcissist himself, how he calculates and plans and manipulates people. Only after spending time in jail did he come to realize what he was and now he writes about how Ns think and operate.

Ns gaslight their "victims" to manipulate reality. They will lie about events, plans, what is actually happening, deflect questions, perform amazing mental sleight of hand, cry with Academy Award winning sincerity, turn around the argument to prove that the victim is wrong and needs therapy, and even go so far as to physically rearrange items like what happened in Alfred Hitchcock's movie, "Gaslight."

A fabulous book on gaslighting is "the gaslight effect" by Dr. Robin Stern who survived her own gaslighting nightmare with a narcissist.

Three Phases of Gaslighting

There are three phases to gaslighting.

A gaslightee knows in Stage One that her version of reality is actually real and uselessly tries to set the record straight by questioning, arguing, screaming, sending emails, texts, and spending hours in useless frustration. For the gaslightee, there are endless questions from obvious "that table is a table not a bus, how can you not see that?" to trying to get indications that the person has a soul, compassion, emotions (besides anger), empathy, love, and so on. But it's pointless because narcissists are caught in a neurological cycle of envy and anger and manipulate events to what is "safe" for them. In other words, they are liars.

Stage Two: Not all narcissists gaslight people. However, once an abuser realizes the power he has to gaslight his victim, his cruelty can be endless. These scenarios may go on daily or weekly. Perhaps all will seem normal for a while and then something happens to "rock the boat" and the drama begins again.

By Stage Three, the gaslightee doesn't trust her own gut, her own reality, and can be depressed, physically ill, and often looks like a raging lunatic to the outside world while her gaslighter continues to Svengali her, continuing to appear charming and gracious and now "patient" with his "crazy" spouse.

There are many women and men who need to know that narcissists aren't just vain people you see on TV shows or celebrities you'll never meet but are everyday people from all walks of life who can and will actively and systematically destroy you for no reason at all except that you're next in line.

Yes, there are already books written about narcissists and gaslighting but they are only obvious to people AFTER they've gone through hell and are

How Many Lies Are Too Many?

trying to figure out what happened after the tornado has swirled away. The average person doesn't know what Narcissism and gaslighting is. We know more about serial killers (who are often extreme NPDs) and schizophrenia then we do about the charming human vampire who will drain us of love and money. We are growing more educated about not falling for cons on the Internet, but that hot guy who pleases your every desire and wants to marry you doesn't seem evil at all.

Spotting the Cracks in the Armor

How can you tell if you're dancing with the devil? Where are the cracks in the armor? These people are MASTERS of disguise, have massive patience in setting the trap, and can live a lie for years without you suspecting a thing. We NEED to tell people, children, teenagers, about this ever growing societal condition before they are lured in. We need to educate people at a young age for navigating human nature is a handy tool to have for any of us.

I've spoken to RCMP officers, police officers and PIs. They say that these con artists are professionals and to never feel stupid about losing your house, your bank account, your heart. NPDs and con artists often know how to stay just within the law enough to take you for everything and there's nothing you can do but move on. I've never heard so much talk about "karma" as I have with the law enforcement officers. They say that karma does happen, that eventually most of these men and women have to pay a price one day. They get cocky and slip and then they are caught. We all know that's how the good shows end.

Disengaging from a narcissist can be a nightmare. They will drag out any break-up process far longer than you could ever dream, to keep you hooked, to drown you, to ruin you financially, emotionally, and sometimes physically. Some women need to go to shelters and change all contact numbers to get away. Most people lose everything including their own children because Ns are fabulous at charming lawyers and shrinks, who are often Ns themselves, making you look insane, which you probably actually are for a while as your grasp on reality is shattered and you can't trust anyone.

There have been a few books published about Psychopaths, NPD, and Gaslighting in recent months. The word is slowly getting out. More need to be written by everyday people so that the concept is out in the mainstream and the average person is educated about how to protect

How Many Lies Are Too Many?

herself or himself. The age of fairy tales provided warnings. There were always disguises, the wolf in sheep's clothing. These warnings have been lost in modern society. People are growing desensitized by technological advances. The amount of damage someone with NPD can do to a regular person is beyond comprehension.

This isn't a matter of a vain manipulator, diva, or a "drama queen." These people are like sharks, well, even sharks likely have emotions. The hardest thing to wrap your mind around is that these people just don't care about you. You are just another cog in their wheel of Narcissistic Supply. When you're used up, there are plenty more to hypnotize. While you're stumbling around in the aftermath of being spit out of their tornado, they've already sucked someone else in. Sure they may contact you acting all friendly, but they just want their Narcissistic Supply from you and likely "want something." The sooner you disengage, the better off you'll be. Unless you enjoy being gaslighted and manipulated.

There are some online forums such as Narcissistic Abuse Recovery Forums, Love Fraud, and Don't Date Him where people share their stories. The common threads in these stories that survivors tell are astounding. So many strange habits from sleeping on the couch, going from sex all the time to nothing, the need for "privacy," threats of leaving, even rudely passing gas. These are common stories that need to be told. These wounded people are crying to be heard, to let the mainstream know that Ns exist and they are dangerous and that you can, in fact, heal yourself in the aftermath.

No Contact

Once you manage to escape from a turbulent life, you need to rebuild. You need to focus on what is ahead of you, not what you've left behind.

There are several types of strategies to utilize in healing. The most important one to stick with is No Contact. And if you're forced to have contact for some reason (like having children together) keep it simple and businesslike.

No contact means that you have no contact with your Gaslighter once you two have split up. Don't be tempted to text or email or phone. This is what they want you to do. Then they'll treat you like dirt when you do. They may toy with you a bit, luring you in with lies but after a while, you'll realize that nothing has changed and nothing ever will.

No contact means no contact. This means that you don't creep Facebook or any other social media keeping track of what your ex is up to. It doesn't matter. That person is dead to you. Move on. Who cares if he talks to your friends? There's nothing you can do. Anything you say just makes you look crazy. Let his true colours come through on their own to them just as it happened to you.

No contact means don't have your friends spy on your ex and report back to you unless you need some kind of court evidence.

No contact isn't for the benefit of your ex. No contact is for the benefit of your own mental health. The less of your brain your ex inhabits, the more of your brain you have to rebuild your life.

Be strong. Don't answer those texts. Don't answer those emails. The ex will use all sorts of tricks to lure you back.

They will feign illness maybe even serious fatal ones.

How Many Lies Are Too Many?

They will say someone in the family is sick or dead.

They will guilt you about the kids.

They will promise to be good.

They will cry huge body wracking tears then dry up a second later as they argue with you.

They will beg.

They will need money.

They have some blackmail material.

They will threaten.

Don't give in. Don't answer. Block them.

Gaslight Shame

Once you realize that you were involved in a gaslight relationship, you might feel depressed or even stupid.

Everyone makes mistakes. Not everyone can recognise the red flags.

The best thing to do is learn from your mistakes and move on.

Remember how it feels in your stomach when something doesn't "feel" right and listen to it from the very beginning.

Don't let the first lie slide.

Don't let anyone have you second guess your perception of reality.

Realize we're all human. Recognize that some people are mentally ill and can't change. Realize that you didn't cause the illness nor can you cure it.

You need to take care of your own mental health after having your reality manipulated.

Remember that even doctors, lawyers and other professionals can be fooled by a pathological liar. You are not alone. There are many under the spell.

Don't expect an apology. If you get it, it will be filled with insincere crocodile tears. The liar blames everyone else, remember? Now you get the blame.

Don't bother trying to explain or get an explanation. It's all lies anyways so why waste your energy?

Journal, paint, draw, dance, write, try new hobbies and interests.

How Many Lies Are Too Many?

Meditate.

Join support groups.

Go to counselling.

Don't blame yourself but be diligent in your choices next time you get involved with someone.

Don't blame yourself or make excuses for his or her behaviour towards you. This person at the very least has issues and at the most, has a dangerous behaviour disorder. You just happened to be in the wrong place at the wrong time. You fell for the lies for whatever reason but the trick is to have a limit, set it and don't stray from it.

Don't blame yourself if you slip. Pick yourself up and move forward again.

Don't fall for ploys to lure you back in. Reconciliations rarely work. You're just wasting valuable time that you could be spending with someone who actually loves you.

Try not to let your entanglement with liars colour your view of life. Not everyone is out to get you. It's normal to be paranoid for a while after a nasty experience. Get help if you find yourself being too paranoid or suspicious of people. However, it's good to take a fresh look around and assess who is truly good for you in your life.

Examples of Gaslighting Lies

David and Jessica have made plans to see a movie on Friday night. They discussed it over dinner on Monday and even talked about which movie to see on Wednesday. However, once Friday rolls around, David says that he never said he was going to a movie. In fact, he has other plans. David leaves. He may or may not answer his phone to Jessica's upset calls. He may play with her mind a bit by making her feel forgetful, stupid and needy.

Lorna and Ralph discuss over the course of the day that they will hit the gym that night. When seven o'clock rolls around, Lorna decides that she's not going. They have a big fight about it as Ralph would have gone right after work if he'd known that Lorna didn't want to go. He insists they had planned the outing and she denies it.

Gaslighting may include slipping drugs or alcohol into food or drink. The Gaslighter may tell the person he or she is ill and give them drugs. They may put a sleeping pill or something else into a drink. Some may even try to poison their lover or put alcohol into the drink of an alcoholic and claim to have forgotten.

Gaslighting may involve taking an item and not owning up to it and perhaps even replacing it days later and declaring to know nothing about it. Or pretending to have lost something when in fact they likely left it somewhere in their cheating travels and then when they go back to get it, it magically "turns up." This can include keys, jewelry, clothes, phones, medical equipment, money, books, baby gear, and so on.

Gaslighting may include picking fights so that the Gaslighter can disappear for hours or days.
Gaslighters make the Gaslightee think he is forgetful, needy, stupid, clingy, suspicious, jealous and possessive when in fact the Gaslightee might just be asking simple questions such as "how was your day?"

How Many Lies Are Too Many?

Gaslighters will close their browsers whenever the Gaslightee is around and say they weren't talking to anyone or surfing porn (creeping old lovers, etc.) even if the Gaslightee saw exactly what they had on their screen seconds earlier.

Gaslighters will erase phone history and claim that suspicious names and numbers have nothing to do with them and it isn't their fault that these people call them.

Gaslighters have secret email accounts, secret profiles on dating and other sites, and generally always pretend to be doing something different than what they really are while on the computer.

If a love letter should slip through the emails, the Gaslighter claims the email was a mistake, either meant for someone else or it's not their fault people love them

Married men and women keep lovers on hooks for years promising to leave their spouses. There's always a benchmark and then a reason why it can't be at that moment. If a person is truly unhappy in a marriage, he or she will leave. If a married person truly loves you more than the spouse, that person will leave the spouse to be with you. Nothing would stop a person in love. Consider how you dance when the person calls? That person doesn't do the same for you. Affairs begin with lies so never believe a word your liar is telling you. Actions speak louder than words. If your lover goes home to the spouse after a magnificent romp with you, your lover isn't leaving the spouse.

Gaslighters always seem to have phone and internet issues. The lines are down, the phone doesn't work, the phone turned itself out, the phone erased the messages, the phone sends messages meant for someone else and so on.

Gaslighters will often go to extreme lengths to keep the lie going. They may have friends lie for them. They may fake phone records, receipts, odometers, internet browsers and so on just so they can make you think you don't know what you're talking about. Even if you catch them red-handed, they will go into full denial punctuated with ignited rage and tears.

If you find strange underwear or condoms, the gaslighter will try to convince you that they are yours and this is just another example about how you forget everything.

Liars often gaslight and lie about pretty much everything. No scenario is too ridiculous or crazy for a liar to spin if it keeps you from guessing the truth. Liars will stop at nothing to keep their victims in the dark about what they are really doing or feeling.

How Many Lies Are Too Many?

Beware of Liars

How many lies are too many?

Some would venture to say it depends what the lie is and why it was told.

Liars always lie.

Never believe you are on the same team as the liar. The pathological liar lies to everyone equally. Just because you are the wife or husband or lover doesn't mean that the liar is confiding in you and only lying to everyone else.

If you know your lover is lying to other people, you can be certain that he or she is lying to you.

If you've ever caught your lover in a lie, don't believe it's going to stop.

If you even suspect your sweetie of cheating, then believe your gut. A few red flags will reassure your gut feelings. Don't wait for a full blown dramatic truth to be unveiled years later. The sooner you get out of the relationship, the better for your emotional and possibly financial health.

Once a cheater, always a cheater. It may take years but a cheater will always find a reason to cheat and can almost always justify it with a pack of lies.

Gaslighters often use tears to deflect attention away from the real discussion.

One lie is too many.

A person who spins lies every day is not a person to trust. You will never be on the same team. You may even commit illegal acts together but your partner will turn on you if push comes to shove. You may be in the middle of being scammed yourself when you think you're scamming someone else. Ever see the movie *The Grifters* about con artists scamming con artists including mother and son? What about *Inception*? Don't believe just because you're related or married or have a child together that you are immune to a lie or a con.

Lying is a personality trait. You know people who lie. Sales people are great liars but the good ones keep the work at work. Do you want to be with someone who will never tell you the truth?

Liars are manipulators. Why are they lying? To get what they want, whatever that may be in that moment. They don't care how their actions affect others. As long as they can steer the truth to how they want to fabricate it, they will.

A person who can't keep his or her promises at the beginning of a relationship will only get worse as time goes on.

A person who lies has no respect for you or anyone else.

A person who lies can be dangerous to you in many ways including psychological, physical and financial.

How many lies are too many?

What is YOUR threshold?

How much do you respect yourself?

How much will you put up with in the name of love?

If you love someone, would you lie to him or her?

If a relationship is built upon trust, there is no room for lies.

How Many Lies Are Too Many?

Take care of your heart, your mind, your soul. Only let healthy, balanced people into your life. Don't pour your time and energy into helping someone who has a history of abuse. There is no winning. Unless there has been years of therapy, a pathological liar will always resort to familiar behaviour.

If you think you love someone too much to leave, consider how much you love yourself?

Why do you think you deserve to be lied to?

Why do you think you deserve to sleep alone every night or wait by the phone for a call that never comes?

Why do you put your life on hold to cater to someone else, only to have him or her lie to you and break your heart?

Give yourself some credit.

You only get one life. Don't waste it on liars. Don't waste it on people who don't care about you. Don't waste it arguing over manipulations of facts. Don't waste it waiting for someone to finally realize that he or she has been acting poorly and will apologize. Don't waste it waiting for married people to leave their spouses. Don't waste it wondering if your lover went where they said they were going.

Live your life to the fullest. Get your bucket list ready. Share it with someone who deserves you.

Love and happiness don't work well with lies.

About the Author

Victoria Summit is a life coach who helps heartbroken clients rebuild their lives.

Gaslight Survivor Series

100 Red Flags in Relationships by Victoria Summit
How Many Lies are Too Many? by Victoria Summit

Printed in Great Britain
by Amazon.co.uk, Ltd.,
Marston Gate.